Storybooks

Wel⌐

Wimzie's House

Written by Wolfgang D. Hoelscher
Illustrated by Mike Duggins, Bill Neville,
& J.J. Rudisill

Carson-Dellosa Publishing Company, Inc.
Greensboro, NC

Library of Congress Card Catalog Number: 99-65000   ISBN 0-88724-461-0

Hi! I'm Wimzie!

I live in a superfantabulous house that's just right for a five-year-old kid like me.

It has lots of places to play and hide, and there are plenty of toys and all sorts of neat stuff. It even has a big backyard and a vegetable garden.

Come on in and I'll show you around!

Welcome to our living room. These are my friends, Horace, Jonas, and Loulou. My grandma Yaya runs a daycare here every day, which is great because my friends can come over and play with me all the time!

Everybody loves the living room because it's where we get together to play or listen to Yaya's stories.

See the little guy on the stairs? That's my baby brother, Bo. You'll meet him later.

Now let's go upstairs so I can show you...

See that airplane hanging in the corner? That's my favorite toy. My mom is an airplane pilot and one day I'll be able to fly a real airplane just like her!

And if you stand on my balcony you can see...

...our beautiful, superific backyard!

We have a toolshed, a picnic table, an apple tree, and a basketball net. And look! There's Horace painting a picture. I'm sure it'll be a beautiful picture because Horace is such a great artist.

Horace is a fantastic friend. He's four years old and loves to draw and paint. Sometimes he's a little shy, but that's okay. Horace is the bravest friend anyone could ever have.

Hey! Let's hurry downstairs because I smell something delicious coming from...

...the kitchen!

I knew it! My grandma Yaya is making her famous double chocolate chip cookies!

Yaya takes care of us all day long, but she still has time to make us treats and tell us stories. She's 150 years old, and she's been all around the world. She was in a rock-n-roll band and she wears sneakers, too. Yaya's the coolest grandma I know!

Wow! What's all that noise coming from the next room?

It's Jonas in the playroom!

This is where we keep most of our toys and there's lots of sunlight with all the windows!

What do you think Jonas is doing?

He's playing with his very special dirt collection, of course! Jonas has a collection of dirt from all sorts of places. My mom brings it to him from the different places she visits in her airplane.

Jonas is five years old and he's my best friend. He's really smart, but that doesn't mean he can't be silly sometimes, too!

Jonas has a little sister. Her name is Loulou. Where could she be hiding?

There she is! Loulou is in Yaya's special closet. It's Loulou's favorite hiding spot and it's a great place for her to play with her dolls. Yaya doesn't mind us being in here as long as we're careful with her old clothes and her rock-n-roll record albums.

Loulou is three years old and she looks a lot like her big brother, Jonas. She's little but that doesn't stop her from doing lots of stuff on her own. She's a great singer and no one can throw a fastball as well as Loulou.

She likes to follow me around a lot, but I don't mind. Sometimes we play dress up and pretend that we're sisters!

Are you ready to meet the rest of my family?

That's my dad, Rousso, in the toolshed. He's a firefighter. He works hard and is very brave. He always has time to play with us when he's not working, though. And he loves to work in his garden when he's not putting out fires.

PEPPERS

My dad has taught me a lot about plants and nature. Thanks to him, I know how important it is for us to plant trees wherever we can!

Guess what! It's time for my mom to come home. Let's go meet her at the front door!

Hooray! She's home!

This is my mom, Graziella. She just returned from another airplane trip. See those wings on her coat? She gets to wear those because she's a pilot. One day, I'll have my own pair of pilot wings, too! I'm sure of it!

My mom is away from home a lot of the time, but I know that she has an important job to do. And when she's home, we have the best times together. She's a super mom!

There's one person left for you to meet.

Do you know who it is?

Bo sleeps in a crib in my room. Sometimes it can be tough sharing a room, but I don't mind that much. It's nice having my baby brother near me—at least when he's being good!

Wait! Do you hear that? Someone is calling me...

It's Yaya! Oh boy! That means it's storytime! We love when Grandma tells us about what it was like a long time ago when she was little like us. Even my mom and dad like to listen.

Sometimes after a long afternoon of playing with my friends, Yaya's stories make me sleepy. But that's not because her stories are boring. I've just had a busy day—like today!

I hope you had lots of fun with me today. You can come over to play whenever you like. I have lots of superific friends, but there's always room for you at my house!

Hurry back soon!